I HAVE STORIES TO TELL

How Cancer Disappeared and A New Womb Appeared

CLAIRE KING WATERTON

Unless otherwise noted, all Scripture quotations are from the King James Version of the Bible.

ISBN: 979-8-9883181-0-1

DEDICATION

This book is dedicated to spreading the continuous miraculous work of the Lord. I will testify as long as God gives me breath. God is still in the business of doing miracles. He is a speaking God and very present help in times of trouble. If people knew just how much Jesus loves them, how life-changing that would be?

PRAYER

My father, my father, as I begin to pray, I bring each and everyone reading this book before your throne in the name of your precious son Jesus Christ. I pray that as people read this book, They will find answer to whatever the need is in their lives. Lord, I pray that healing and deliverance will be manifested. I pray Isaiah 54:17 that no weapon that is formed against them shall prosper. I send back every arrow of sickness that was fired back to the sender. Let healing begin in your spirit, every cell of your blood, every bone of your body, and fiber of your being. Let God's word saturates your spirit, mind and body, leaving no room for any sickness or disease. I pray a lifting in your life and that your health aligns to the prescribed order of God in Jesus's mighty name. You are untouchable and unkillable to sickness. You are like He is right now in the mighty name of Jesus, Amen. Jeremiah 17:14, 1 Peter2:24, Psalms 147:3, James 5:16

CONTENTS

01

THE BEGINNING

In early November of 2020, I started seeing signs that something was wrong. I had gone through menopause, so I knew the blood flow wasn't normal. I ended up in the emergency room and was told it may be what came across my mind. The young doctor looked so worried that I already knew the news was not good before she said anything. As I sat there waiting for her, I had a lot on my mind then she came back after asking a lot of questions and said it might be a sign of cancer. I left there that night, vowing that I was healed and it was not cancer. Anyway, I received results from the hospital but not anything about that. Time went on and all signs stopped. I was convinced that was over with, and I had nothing to worry about.

I told my daughter, who was in medical school at the time. She insisted that I go ahead and get another checkup at Weill Cornell hospital in Manhattan. I did another round of tests there and was sent for a biopsy. The result came back negative, and because the bleeding had stopped, I was so happy with the result. The doctors had me do a sonogram, the one with the camera, twice. What they saw and what the results said didn't match. They were not happy and insisted on further examination. I didn't take them seriously. I went ahead with my plans.

My mom was very sick, left the US went home to Guyana. My eldest sister went to take care of her. In May I joined her to help with my mom. The first couple of months everything seems fine, kept myself busy taking great care of my mom.

I started noticing the blood again but not as much as it was before. I tried to brush it off, but I knew this was bad. I was able to keep a straight face not giving no signal that something was wrong. The last thing I wanted was for my mom to know I was sick. She had enough on her plate.

The blood came and went, it seems like if I did too much it was there, I was very uncomfortable and worried but did not get back on the plane.

The doctors called many times while I was in Guyana, at one point I stopped answering the phone, because it was beginning to be obvious. The next thing I knew my daughter started calling me, advising me to leave Guyana and return, my doctor had gotten in contact with her. I refused to leave my mom until she passed on August 8th.

Appointments were made before I got back to the US, upon my arrival there were so many appointments. I was overwhelmed. I had done a biopsy before I went to Guyana, a new one was ordered along with more test.

I remember as I finished the biopsy, a terrible fear came over me. I can't explain it but I knew it was bad news. The technician told me the doctors would call me in ten days' time, to my surprise the doctor called me I believed was the next day. I was so shocked.

It was explained to me by the doctor on the phone. What I heard her say it's like I had a choice, I had an IUD inserted in me before I left for Guyana. I was told initially than would prevent the thickness of the lining of my uterus turning to endometrial cancer. So, when she called me, it sounded like it wasn't so bad I could have left it in for a year, after one year if the thickness increases then they will decide.

The doctor explained to me, but it seems like I convinced myself I heard something else. I didn't follow up with my appointments. Was that wisdom? No, it wasn't. I would see the doctor's calling and ignore them. It was fear. I was afraid of what I was going to hear.

In early October, the heavy bleeding started. I kept it to myself. In November of that year, after the hospital could not get in contact with me, they called my daughter.

Now I had told her something else according to what I understood, but the doctors told her it was endometrial cancer. I was just about to have dinner when she came from downstairs after speaking to the doctor. The way she looked, I knew, wasn't good. She just came out with it. "Mom, you have cancer." My husband and I couldn't eat another spoon of that food. We just left, staring into space, and said nothing more. That night I didn't sleep. I cried all night. It was why me? Why now? I had just lost my mom in August; I was still in grief much less dealing with my own situation so seriously. The very next day I said to myself I can go like this, or I can believe God for healing. So, I decided to believe this God that I serve.

My daughter and I went to the next appointment together. She said she wanted to be there to hear all the details herself. The doctors did all sorts of exams, including a pelvic exam, which was normal. My daughter took the report, and she asked the doctors lots of questions, but the one that had concerns was that there were two types of cancer. I think it cauterized as A or B, B being the worse, and of course, I had B, which indicated that the cancer was aggressive. I said to her I don't care what the doctors were saying I know I'm healed; she said, you said your mom was healed and she died. A righteous indignation rose in me and I said I shall live and not die. The fight has now begun.

02

DEALING WITH FEAR

I had to reality-check my whole life. I discovered I always had a fear of getting cancer. I know the only fear that I am permitted to have is the fear of God. I would confess with my mouth, but my heart was full of fear. Fear, if not dealt with will cripple you. I had faith I know God is God and I had proven him so many times. I know and sing he is a miracle-working God, but that is the problem. There should not be a but. When you pray, believe, don't change your mind. Just believe, and be as a child when it comes to believing God.

Around that period, believers that I knew personally died with that same cancer. A sister friend confided in me that she had cancer in the same area as I. You won't believe I encouraged her, believed, and prayed for her but I never told her that I was going through the same thing. I used to send scriptures and links for her to go on for prayers. She went home to be with the Lord without knowing about a similar situation I had. To people, faith can mean different things. People talk about one thing, but, in their heart, only God knows what they really believe. Somehow, I knew that death wasn't my portion; I wasn't going down like that. Fear and faith do not go together, so I decided one had to go completely, and that was fear. My faith is my confidence in this great God whom he has proven himself over and over again.

There's a point in your life when you must ask yourself, what do you know about God? It is not what my pastor says about God. It's what you know about GOD. It's who you know God to be in your personal and public life. The people that know their God shall do exploit. Let the personal revelation about God bring you out of that situation. My confidence is in the name of the Lord. I had encounters with God. The Holy Ghost would remind me giving me strength, so I marched on with faith. What God says stands. It does not matter how many people died with the same condition. I am not dying. Tell yourself you are God's favorite. I am special.

What God did not give to me I didn't want, the spirit of fear I rejected, the spirit of faith I embraced. Fear torments and reminds you about defeat and death. Faith gives you hope and allows you to see yourself healed in the spirit, so your physical bodies manifest that healing. The word of God says that perfect love cast away fear John 4:18. People you cannot believe God in fear, think upon things that are pure, holy and of good report. I use my pass miracles that God performed and others that I also witnessed, people's testimonies. God also spoke to me so many times through his word. The holy ghost once told me this sickness is not unto death.

Do you know every night, if I wasn't praying, I was sleeping very sound? I was not going to lose my sleep. No, faith lets you sleep. I'm God's beloved, and he promised me sleep. I did lose weight because I fasted a lot which I needed to, but when I wasn't fasting, I was eating. Even then, fasting was a challenge. I didn't lose my appetite. I didn't put my life on hold. I spent time planning; I have a destiny to fulfill and a purpose on earth. I am not going back to my Father with unfinished business, no Sir. Our 40th wedding anniversary was in December, and the devil kept telling me I would not be able to celebrate, but the devil is a liar. We know for sure.

03

GET RID OF UNFORGIVENESS

Now when you have something as serious as cancer, aggressively spreading in your body, you must decide whether you live or not. My mind was clear. The word of God said I have life and death in my mouth. There is life power in my mouth and death power in my mouth. I will use life because I chose it, so first thing first, is to get your priorities right, which means your life right. David said search me, oh God, and know my heart today, see if there be any wicked way in me. I searched myself and knew I had unforgiveness, and had to let go of people and stuff that weighed me down.

Unforgiveness will block your healing. It's too heavy a weight to carry. Maybe if you check the reason why you are sick or perhaps why you are not seeing your healing. Be truthful to yourself and get rid of things that are holding you back. It is not worth it. The truth is not all people that proclaim the name Jesus knows who Jesus is, so my thing is you can love everyone, but you don't have to like them or let them near you. In other words, love them from afar. You owe people love, not access INTO YOUR LIFE. I'm learning not all Christians are nice. You can find the meanest people greeting people at churches, answering even the church phones, and in prayer groups, so love people as God commands you. You are commanded to love them but not permitted to trust anyone. As a matter of fact, if I remember clearly, the Bible says we should only trust God.

When I was younger and young in Christ, whenever I met Christians, I was so happy thinking all is well because I'm thinking we are one in the spirit, one in the Lord, but I learned there are so many different types of Christians. You need the spirit of wisdom and discernment or you can be hurt badly by so-called Christians.

I constantly checked with God to ensure my heart was right, and I can truly say that God helped me very much. Please don't allow unforgiveness to stop your healing. You may feel you are blessed and things are still alright, but sometimes only God's mercy that is extended to you. Forgive and let go. It's amazing to see how many Christians are walking around, bruised by the church and living in unforgiveness. Set yourself free. Shake it off. The only person who unforgiveness hurts is you. The weight of it is too heavy a load to carry. Stop giving people so much power over you. Find the strength to move on. If I'm finding it difficult to let something go, I ask God to help me, and He does.

How would you know you have forgiven someone? It's when that person's name comes up in any conversation and you don't participate by saying anything bad. Never have anything bad to say. No, do not warn anybody. In fact, if the person needs help and you are in a position to help them and not with pride like you see who has to help you now. No, leave things to God. He is big enough to handle your interest. Ephesians 4:31-32

04

FAITH. FAITH. FAITH

God says it is impossible to please him without faith. You cannot serve a God that you can't see without faith. Impossible. You need faith to pray. You need faith for everything. Being a Christian, we live a faith-based life. The word also says the just shall live by faith. Faith has dimensions, I would say. Ephesians 6:16 says, above all, taking the shield of faith, wherewith you shall be able to quench the fiery darts of the wicked. Faith is the most important part of the armor of protection. The Bible says above all the rest of very important parts of the armor. It is your faith. Once your faith is tampered with, your Christian life is affected; therefore, whatever you are trusting God for in trouble, in my case, would have been my healing. Your faith must be unshakable. It is in who you believe. God is unshakable and loves when you boast in Him. The song says he has a track record of keeping his word. He is not about to stop doing it now.

We all can probably coat a scripture about faith. It is easier to talk about faith than to use it. I always want to be known as a woman of strong faith; I have proven God in many ways. God has come through for me big time in difficult situations, so I am a faithy person, lol. I just came up with that word, you can have faith, but do you know that every situation is different? Faith is a fight. Hold your ground, not caring what your eyes see or how your body feels. Faith doesn't mind how big the mountain is before you. It just stays in agreement with the word of your father. My father says I'm healed, then I'm healed, and let it settle in your heart. Shield your heart with it. If God was to heal everyone as soon as they pray, and healing manifests right away, it would seem as though everyone has faith. We all know that's not how it works all the time. God does things however he pleases. It may be instant. It may be later. It may be yes. It may be no. Some people get healed supernaturally, and some get healed through medicine.

One thing I can say is it's a battle of the mind. My mind might be saying something at the moment, but I didn't allow that to process through my lips. It didn't matter how I was feeling or what didn't change when I expected it to. I held my thought and did not allow my thought to change my confession, strong faith does not mean doubts wouldn't come, but you square your shoulders and hold your confession. The benefit of not sharing with others is apart from the devil reminding you. This thing is in your body. You do not have people calling to talk about sickness, except 3 people that knew I was sick. I had no one else calling to check up on me. I didn't have constant conversations about that. In fact, I never talked about cancer with anyone except the doctors, and even then, I would tune out what they were saying. I never accepted it. I dressed well so I wouldn't appear sick, made certain my continence was in check, and kept my faith. I talked to my father constantly and believed him. I believed he loved me enough to heal me, oh my precious father.

Now to know if you have faith, you have to be tested, some tests will not be pleasant, and some may be life-threatening, but you must take a chance on faith. I notice in the Bible, you are only asked to have faith as small as a mustard seed to move mountains. Think about this mustard seed. It is so small it probably took more faith to accept a God that you have never seen to your knowledge, never did anything for you in most cases. You are now being introduced to this God. What am I trying to say? If you have faith to believe there is a God that loves you and sent his only begotten son to die for you, then it's not that hard to believe he cares enough to heal you and has good intentions for you.

I thought there were many kinds of faith. Matthew 8:26 talks about little faith. I never thought about this until now; Hebrews 11:1 says faith is the substance of things, hope for evidence of it not seen. That's the definition of faith. Whether small or big, it's faith in God, hoping without evidence. Then there is great faith. We all want to be here, but do you know you must be tried to know how great your faith is? In the situation with the centurion man, his faith marveled Jesus. Jesus said to him in Matthew 8:5-10. I have not seen so great faith, no, not in Israel. The Bible never said that man was with Jesus before then but, yet he had so much faith. We weren't told the man's name, meaning he was certainly not a disciple or apostle or such, but he had so much faith. That man probably had more faith than the people with him, seeing all the miracles Jesus performed. I think if that man had been in the boat when the storm came, he would have told them to be calm. Do you see who is in the boat? We are good. Let Jesus sleep.

In 2 Peter 1:5, there are other things that you should add to your faith. If you have faith to move the biggest mountain and you don't add these things on top of faith, you may never get healed. One of these things is love. I'm not going through all, but you can go to Second Peter and read the rest. I'm using love as an example. The Bible says if you have faith to move mountains but no love, your faith is useless, and you are nothing. I am looking at 1 John: 4:7-8 but most of this chapter explains Love, and what I'm seeing is it explains God. He is love. So how can you have faith in love and you don't have love?

Faith without works is dead. Having faith is not enough. God has given each of us a measure of faith, but you must build up yourself in the Holy Ghost by speaking in tongues. Faith comes by hearing the word of God. That doesn't mean going to church on Sundays and hearing a sermon. No, it means every chance you have, whatever means you have but a listener of the word. I am a firm believer in listening and studying the word and allowing God to reveal and speak to me through his word. Our daily priority should be spending time in the word. Remember, that's the easiest way to hear God.

05

PRAY IN YOUR HEAVENLY LANGUAGE

The gift of tongues is not a gift to be put in a corner. God has given us this unique gift for a purpose. We all have our own earthly language which we can pray with, but the God of all knowledge taught it wise to bless us with another language to speak to Him. Now let us think about that. Let that sink in. Ask yourself what it is for. In Jude, one twenty says we build ourselves up when we speak in tongues. Some prayers can't be uttered in your language, sometimes our human self can't explain what it is we want relayed to our Father. Sometimes we groan but speaking in tongues is our heavenly language to our Father.

Jude 20 building up yourself in the most holy faith. How? By speaking in the Holy GHOST. There will come a time when believing is not enough, just know your God. I know God. I don't just believe there is a God somewhere. No, this God exists in me. He talks to me, and I talk to Him. Daniel 10:31 those who know their God are the ones that will do exploits. God's people are destroyed not because they lack faith but knowledge.

We live in a very spiritual world. The word of God says we wrestle not against flesh and blood but against principalities and rulers of darkness. This world is more spiritual than physical, believe me.

If you know the story of how Daniel's answer was delayed because the devil understood Daniel's prayer and tried to stop his prayer from being answered. Daniel's prayer was answered from the first day he prayed, but the prince of the kingdom of Persia prevented the angel from carrying the answer for 21 days. The angel explained how Michael, one of the chief princes, had to go help him so he could deliver the answer to Daniel.

We must know the devil does not know anything about what you are praying about when we pray in tongues. It's our heavenly language that is a language between you and your Father. Feel free to become very talkative in the spirit. I found out I pray more now in tongues than anything else doesn't matter where I am. Tongues are for warfare. When you are sick with something as serious as cancer, you have to do warfare prayer, and for me, that was done in tongues.

06

RECOGNIZE THE THIRD VOICE

You don't have to be sick to know there's always a third voice. It's God's voice, your voice, and the devil's voice. When you receive a bad report from the doctor right away, guard your thoughts. Don't allow the loudest voice to win. Remember the saying the empty barrel makes the most noise. Let noise be just noise. Stay in tune for the still-sound voice. Remember, God, has given you a sound mind because his voice is sound and cannot be mistaken. The voice of the Lord brings calmness, sobriety, and tranquility. It does not confuse you nor bring fear to you. It always gives you answers, even under pressure. The devil will always tell you something opposite to what God says in His word. He is easy to recognize. He is not your friend; he doesn't want to be your friend. He wants to take you out. Hear me today. Even if you are not serving God, the devil still doesn't like you. As a matter of fact, if you are his agent from hell, he still doesn't love you. He doesn't have the ability to love. God is love, and out of His love flows healing and compassion for you.

I looked for healing scriptures and equipped myself with them. The only way to quiet the third voice is to use the word of God. Hebrews 4:12 The word of God is quick and powerful, and sharper than any two-edged sword, piercing even to the dividing asunder of soul and spirit. The word of God is God himself. Another thing is to know how powerful the name of Jesus is and tell yourself everything and everyone has to bow at the feet of Jesus. I remember sometimes in the night, as soon as I turned or got up to use the bathroom, there came the third voice, remember, you have cancer. You are going to die. It's just going to get worse. Remember, this person died of that same cancer. The worse was, why would you trust God when you don't know if He will heal you? Look how many Christians died believing God was going to heal them. I tell you the truth that had me for some time asking quietly was God going to heal me. What makes me different?

One opportunity to speak to my dad without reservation. I began speaking to my Father, and God is so loving. I tell you, it's beautiful to be speaking to God and hearing Him speak back to you. God told me I was going to write this book and many other books; I asked him, a book, Lord? He said yes, and I picked up my iPad that night and started writing. I wrote like I was already healed. I had so much joy that night writing. God had told me before that I would write a book, but I thought it was about something else He had delivered me from. I had a good conversation with my Father. I started writing this book by faith. At that time, I was confessing I was healed without any evidence, blood still flowing, but I'm the just, and by my faith, I live. God told me a lot of things that night, and I remember how happy I was. I knew God had heard my prayer, and I felt all His attention was on me, and He cared, oh yes, He cared. Jesus. Jesus, oh, how He loves me so, and I just love him back. Oh yeah, I do.

I had to determine that come what may, I would believe in God. I went into fasting and praying. I don't know the number of days, but I had to hear from God. I know God had delivered me from something big before, and I also knew there was and is nothing too hard for Him. I would talk to him and tell Him some things I don't care to repeat. I told Him because I knew He loves me and cares for me, and He wouldn't let me down, and He wasn't about to tell anyone else what I said. I don't know if anyone has experienced this, but sometimes during prayer, thoughts would come, and I would be shocked and must rebuke the devil. The devil won't give up, so you have to speak louder than him. When you continually rebuke him, he will eventually flee from you.

07

TAKE HEALING BY FORCE

I had to learn to pray, don't mind how I was feeling, it wasn't I don't feel like praying today or I'm busy no, it was praying until something happened. I prayed and when it seemed like my prayer was not being answered I prayed more. If I may say when you pray, remember you are praying to your dad who loves you dearly and whose thoughts for you are good.

Check scriptures to see how much He loves you, more than that look around and see His goodness around you. Stand strong thinking how your earthly father who some of them does not even know God but would kill to save you, how much more your father of all fathers who sent His only son to die so you might walk in health. I asked God to hug me on different occasion and guess what He did i asked Him to show me signs guess what He did, I can't speak for anyone else, but I found out while I was sick how much patience and love God has for me.

Don't ever leave your healing to the dependence of people praying for you or intercessory groups, no be your own prayer warrior, be your own intercessor, we have been made priest unto our God we can go to God ourselves, people have their own problems, yes, we still need to always pray for each other. Job 42: 10 the Lord restored Job after he prayed for his friends, it is hard to pray for others effectively constantly when you yourself have a life challenge, but you still must do it.

Sometimes people may not see you or your problem, your sickness or whatever case as important as you do. I realize I cannot be lazy with my prayer I learned to pray and forget time. At one time in my life, one-hour prayer I felt was a great accomplishment now it's just beginners' prayer for me. I heard and seen the life of the people I follow, how they pray for hours and hours every day and that's where I want to be. I don't want to be praying for any selfish reason except to know Gods voice and to be in His presence more than anything else. If you stay in the presence of God how can sickness stay? Just tell me How. Don't be timid with your prayers, you have power over death.

Pray violent prayers, be violent with your prayers, cancer aggressive you be more aggressive. I say pray like the Africans, Matthew 11-12 the violent take it by force, you are not playing with the devil, he sure isn't playing with you, he is out to kill you. The devil is here to kill, to steal and to destroy. He is the accuser of the brethren; he is going before God making accusations against us but thank God Jesus is on the right side of the father making intercession for us. We are praying from a seated position, yes, a position of power and strength. We are seated in heavenly places in Christ Jesus, God gives us power so we can subdue powers. God gives us power to cast out sickness. Lay hold on the power God has given you, you can't be what God wants you to be without power. I love the scripture that says, the same spirit that raised Jesus from the dead it is that same spirit lives in me woooooh, that is God's spirit. Now tell me who can battle with the Lord.

Do you know your joy irritates the devil, he expects you to be sorrowful and afraid as he throws darts at you. God say the joy of the Lord is your strength so in keeping your joy the devil is defeated. Joy throws the devil off because when he shoots arrows at you, he waits for your reaction so by keeping your joy he is seeing strength and that's not what he expects. The devil's intention is for your reaction to look like a defeated foe but what he would see is strength. When the devil sees your joy, it tells him this one knows who she is, she knows she walks in victory, I can't mess with her. Have your joy overflow, let it overflow in your life. It is one of the fruits of the spirit, lack of it can even make you sick. Romans12:12 be joyful in hope, patient in affliction, faithful in prayer. Psalm 94:19 says When anxiety was great within me, your consolation brought me joy.

08

LEARN TO BE QUIET

In first Thessalonians 4:11, the apostle Paul told the Thessalonians they should study to be quiet; do you know in your quietness how much you can learn? When you are quiet, you will hear God clearly and get instructions. Ecclesiastes 3;7 says there is a time to keep silent and there is a time to speak. James 1:19 says slow to speak. I heard the news I told my husband and one sister, who I knew would go on her knees before God. I chose not to say anything to my children or siblings; it was not easy, but I believed God wanted me to be quiet.

I have a sister that had a problem with her breast for years. She was scheduled for surgery. Whatever the explanation, the doctor said she had to do surgery. The breast was leaking puss and causing severe pain. She said sometimes the breast would be pulling with pain so bad. Anyway, the night before the surgery, she packed the things she would need to use in the hospital but was waiting on one nightgown from the tailor. However, that wasn't finished, and she decided not to go for the surgery but trust God.

She told my mom in the morning that she was not going anymore. My mom, a believer, also agreed she should trust God on this. Years went by. She was there believing God would heal her but didn't say anything to anyone. Many friends right in the area died one after the other with breast cancer. She said she didn't tell anyone else, not even me. She said hearing about people dying of breast cancer with what was happening to her was hard.

She came to the United States in November of 2018, I believe, and two weeks after, she and her husband accompanied me to a conference with Apostle Johnson Suleman, which was kept in the Bronx, New York, two days before Thanksgiving. There were two services per day, we attended the first one, which was very good, and I wanted to leave because I had so much to do before Thanksgiving. My brother-in-law said he thought we /should wait; we were already there, and I thought hesitant. I stayed, I thought but hesitantly I stayed. I thank God I did that night. OMG, yes, that night, not only did God show up for my sister, but He also showed up for me too.

I was sitting there. The worship had just finished, and Apostle came on, and the very first thing he said was Claire; God said I should pray for Claire, with shock I didn't get up right away, so my sister, who was sitting a little distance from me shouted for me to go forward which I did. He told me to the point why I was there, but I am not speaking here about me, so then he said the lady with the black and white scarf around her neck, which was my sister, as she was walking down the aisle, he asked her who has a son named Ken? Her eldest son's name is Ken, among other things. He told her to put her hands across her chest and said God said that would not kill you. Since then, my sister has taken a yearly mammogram, and all is well to the Glory of God.

I learned in this process, you cannot tell everyone everything. James 1:19 says be slow to speak, choose people of the same faith believing the same thing, not doubting. I learned some people are agents of bad news, whether bringing or carrying. You can tell people your problem but tell yourself only God knows the heart of men. Would this person pray, or would you be the latest news? Then another thing is that you are confessing you are the healed and all the faith-filled confession, but unknowing to you, the people that should be praying for you are the ones who make your condition a topic in a negative way. My pastor says the devil will sabotage you when you talk too much.

I learned from God that not everyone will pray for you. Trust God, not the flesh. I won't allow any and everyone to lay hands on me nor pray for me. If I'm insignificant to pray with you, then I'm insignificant for you to pray for me. I will say I don't like people praying for me who do not like me.no, no, no. I love people, and I love the God in people, but sometimes people just don't click, and its nothing wrong with that. We all have different paths.

People being sorry for you will not bring healing. Stay quiet in the presence of the Lord. Stop talking too much. Everybody knows your business, the person that you are sharing with. Will they help you, or what you are informing them about will it help them in any way?

I stayed in my bedroom fasting and praying until healing manifested. Doing that will teach you to move your mind away from your problems and enjoy God's presence. I cut off social media and turned your phone off. Sometimes you will hear in your spirit, don't answer your phone or turn your phone off. You can talk to that person later. Make people's business theirs. I can't tell you how much I don't want to hear others' business. We are too caught up with the world. Jesus is coming soon. Let's turn our attention to what God is saying. Make Him a priority, period.

09

BE THANKFUL

Be careful to give thanks, develop a thankful heart not when all is well, and be always thankful. Is it easier said than done? Yes, that's why you have to purpose to be thankful, always see someone else struggles worse than yours, tell yourself that person is on a hospital bed, and you are walking free. Tell yourself that people can't eat. You can. Find little things to be thankful for, and read inspiring books. My mom died the same year I was diagnosed with this aggressive cancer. I was fortunate to be with her for almost four months of the eight that she was sick. Not one day she complained, she trusted God until her end, but she never looked for pity. She was more concerned with her children and grands. She was very thankful for her over 80 years on earth.

After my mom passed, I went into the bedroom to pray, and I began to praise and give thanks. I knew it was important for me to give thanks to my God even though it didn't work out how we had hoped. I also knew that it was time to do what I sang about and give him thanks in the good times and the bad times. I felt every fiber of my being as I praised and worshiped that day, but God is to be Praised, come what may.

Reading inspirational books encourages you to stay strong, and you will see some people who have gone through the worse and how God brought them out. Even in books, God answers you and instructs you. His instruction gives you light, guidance, and answers. The word of God is spirit and life. It would feed your spirit. Once healing reaches your spirit, your body will manifest healing. First, receive it in your spirit then it will manifest physically.

Faith comes by hearing the word of God. The word is God himself. I remember thinking to myself, God's spirit lives in me. How can sickness live in me? They cannot dwell together. The word of God says the same spirit that raised Jesus from the dead resides in me, one is all-powerful, and the other comes from the one with borrowed power that is subjected to the all-powerful. I knew the weaker had to leave. The word of God says I am as He is right here in this world, not the world to come, no this world. We have power over every disease and another thing. Stop making cancer a big deal. Use that time to show how big God is. Shout Hallelujah!

Psalms 95;6 Says come let us worship and bow down, let us kneel before the Lord, our maker, for He is our God, we are the people of His pasture and the sheep of His hand. Do you know that, above all things, worship is more important? God comes and communes with us in worship. He loves when we adore Him with Praise.

Ask yourself this question. How can you love on someone and not reap the benefits? That can't happen. God wants us to tell Him how great He is, how marvelous and spectacular, He is our one and only and such like. I love to say to Him there is no me without Him. I would say, God, you know I only know you. I have never turned to no other God but you. I know no other. As far as

I'm concerned, there is no other God but you. You are the pillar that holds my life, you are always here with us, and I thank you.

10

DON'T DESPISE PROPHECY

The Bible says believe the prophet and you shall prosper 2 Chronicles 20:20 The Amplified Version says believe and trust in His prophets and succeed. In the New Testament, it says despise, not prophesying, for it is the will of God. In 1 Corinthians 14:3 prophecy is for edifying the church. We are the church.

In the olden days, even the kings sought the prophets, in 2 Kings 5, remember when the young girl told her master Naaman to go seek help from the prophet Elisha, and it turned out he got healed after obeying the prophet's instruction? The part that touches me is how confident the young maid was that if he only visited the prophet, all would be well. It had to be she knew her God of the Israelites. I feel the same way today about true prophets because of the testimony of my encounters with the prophet's souls are saved.

In first Samuel 28; 1-3, King Saul even sought answers from Samuel while he was in the grave. Prophets are the mouthpiece of God himself. God chose those people for that particular task, and they are set apart. I think it was the prophet Elisha; when the Israelites were burying a man, the body touched Elisha's bones, and the dead man came alive. What? Yes, powerful. I really love prophets. Every encounter for me with a prophet was remarkable. Can I say this? Word of knowledge is not a prophecy. It is either you are a prophet, or you are not. I hate it when people generalize prophecy. God says He will make you great. Anyone can say that. Nothing profound. Stop, stop, stop. Please stay in your lane. Only God can call you to be a prophet.

Some people do not like to hear about prophets. Well, I'm here to testify that my healing came through a prophet whom I highly esteem. If you ask me, everyone needs a prophet. Yes, I have a very good Pastor, but there are situations that need a prophet's anointing. It's not an argument for me to believe what you want, but for me, whenever I had a situation that was very serious and seemed to be going nowhere, it didn't matter how I prayed and fasted. God used a prophet to deliver me. I think even pastors need prophets over them. A true prophet sees and hears directly from God. They not only speak what God says to you, but they speak, and God backs them up.

During this time and even way before, I would stay up and pray with Apostle Johnson Sulemon. It was during the pandemic he started what he called wonders without numbers. Every night from 12am until after 1am, he would come on YouTube and pray live. I would pray almost every night for over a year, even until now. One night as he was praying, he stopped and said that God said He was healing someone of cancer. I shouted, "That's me, now" Apostle Suleman didn't call my name, but I held on to what God said. I believed I was the one God was talking to. The devil, of course, tried to put doubt saying maybe it wasn't me, but I held on to that prophecy for dear life.

I continued to see the same symptoms, but I believed God. I held onto my confession; I was healed. The doctors decided they were going to do surgery to remove my womb and ovaries. I agreed but secretly waited to hear when God said don't go for surgery. I went for so many tests leading up to the surgery date, but nothing showed that the cancer had gone, but I remain confident in Jesus.

The surgery date was set for March 15, 2022. As the date came close, I asked God one day. You said I'm healed. Please stop this bleeding. The next day the blood stopped. Wow, God, so why am I going for surgery if I am healed? To be honest, I got frustrated. We have to realize God will surprise us every time His ways are not our ways. We think we understand God, but we will never understand Him. He is sovereign. His thoughts are higher than ours. Don't try putting God in a box. You never can. I had to learn patience, and God doesn't take bribes. Ha, Ha! If I tell you what I told God one time but learn how much God loves me, yes me. Oh, and I will never stop loving Him.

The day before the surgery, it was so quiet in our home. It normally is quiet, but there was such a stillness I was left alone for a moment in the room, which I needed so badly to talk to my Father. I closed the door, sat up on my bed, and began to talk to my Father. I asked Him if I was healed, then why I was going to do this surgery? And the loving Father He is, He answered me. I remember how quickly God answered me as if he was waiting, knowing how I felt and wanting to speak to me. My Father said to me, go to Psalms 46 and read it. I said Psalms 46. He said yes. I opened my Bible and read. The scripture started with God is my refuge and strength, a very present help in trouble, but when I got to verse 10, that's where my answer was. He will be exalted among the heathen; how will He be exalted throughout the earth? He has to show off himself. How will the unbelievers know there is a God? If they cannot see miracles. I got happy. My Dad said, be still and just watch me do this. I felt light. I knew all was well. I felt the presence of God. I felt loved like I never felt before.

O, how he loves me so! This God that I know is faithful to the end, He will never leave me nor forsake me. I will never forget that experience. God came down in my bedroom just to let me know I was and would be ok.

Listen to me. If you are serving a god and he is mute, ask him what's up. In times like these, you need a God you can talk to and get answers, A God who will not leave you hanging. This God I have known and accepted since the age of 11 has never let me down. Did I let him down? Oh, many times! Did he give up on me? Never. I say to anyone reading this book who has not personally accepted Jesus as Lord, go ahead and give him a try. You will never regret it.

11

DON'T FORGET THE PRAISE

It takes faith and a knowing to praise God in every situation. Praise Him in advance. Be happy. God loves when we come to him in confidence. Go to church and dance, in your home dance, in your car, sing. I remember the Sunday before the surgery. I danced in church like nobody's business. No one knew I was going for surgery. Praise breaks forth your victory. Praise backs down the devil and surprises him. He thought he had ambushed you in a corner, but you will not fall backward. You will arise and go forth in the name of Jesus.

Psalms 28;7 says The Lord is my strength and my shield; my heart trusts in him, and he helps me. My heart leaps for joy, and with my song, I praise him.

Praise is when we talk about God, shout about how good he is. Praise him in spirit of. It's a sacrifice Psalms 54:6- it is confidence in the God you serve. Revelations 4:11 Praise is for God's pleasure; we give our God pleasure by worshipping him. God is worthy to be praised. He lives in our Praise and works miracles in our Praise.

When the children of Israel shouted with Praise, the wall of Jericho came down.

Praise will bring you out of whatever situation you are in, Praise creates an atmosphere where healing is manifest. Your victory may be waiting on your Praise.

The song says to count your blessings and name them one by one, and it will surprise you what and how much the Lord has done. It pays to sit back sometimes and meditate on God and allow the Holy Spirit to take you back things you forgot. With time, the spirit of the living God will bring the goodness of God back to you, reminding you how God has been good to you throughout the years. Things I forgot when the Holy Spirit brings them back to me, it melts my heart and always when I need to remember. Oh God, you are so good to me. You must love me so much. There is always something to praise God for. My eyes well up with tears just thinking of the ways God has been good to me.

Lately, when I begin to even think about praising or worshipping God, tears just flow for no reason. It's an awesome thing to have fellowship with God. Let not what you see with your naked eyes around you that is discouraging make you doubt God. Remember, not everything you will understand. Just trust the process. Praise, Praise, Praise.

12

THE POWER OF CONFESSION

Never change your confession

Daily confession-confession is powerful – the words we speak are spirit and life. When we speak, the words go out and form life or death. The words itself is spirit that goes and performs that miracle in your body.

The word is working in me.

I refuse to be sick; sickness has no business with me.

Greater is he that is in me than he that is in the world.

Greater is he that is in me than this sickness in me.

God is able to do exceedingly abundantly above all I ask or think, according to the power that worketh in me - Eph 3:20

With long life, will he satisfy me - Psalms 91:16

There shall no evil befall me.

I have the life and nature of God.

I am more than a conqueror.

I am the seed of Abraham.

I have divine health.

I am the healed of the Lord.

I will rest in promises.

My strength is renewed daily.

I am a child of the King.

Victory is mine, I am victorious.

I refuse to be sick; sickness has no business with me.

13

THE MIRACLE

I left home with all confidence that all is well and arrived about 5am as I was told. I went through all the preparations and was placed in the waiting room. The lead doctor came into the room. She looked more nervous than ever. She said while rubbing my hands, you must be so afraid. I answered with such boldness that could have only come from GOD. I SAID: "NO, I'M READY WHEN YOU ARE." She was in shock. I guess she didn't expect that, and we both started laughing. I went into surgery and came out with everything removed: my womb and ovaries. They had a room prepared for me to stay at least overnight. This was a major surgery, and my blood pressure went up during the surgery. They were very surprised I recovered so well. I was sent home the same day. I was given a date of March 30 to return for the results. I was so confident that I was healed. God told me when I returned to the doctors they would tell me I have no cancer and that I should ask them was cancer found?

I had about five cuts on my tummy. They all healed well. The day of my appointment came. I went there with boldness and was very happy, but as I was sitting there, everyone was called, and I was left sitting there all by myself. My mind started to go in all directions, and my heart started fluttering and this fear tried to take me over. I said to my Father, God, please, I need your peace right now, and GOD SAID TO ME, get your phone. I took my phone out of my bag. He said go to what's app? I went there, and I saw three messages two were from a ministry that I support and a video from my cousins. I opened the one from my cousin, whom I didn't speak to for a very long time. The video was a little boy singing a reggae song,' Baby, don't worry about a thing because every little thing going to be alright.... listen, if you were somewhere watching me, you would have thought I was crazy. I laughed so hard. I felt God's peace come and take over. Trust me. God has a sense of humor.

Right about the same time, the doctor came to get me as I sat on the chair. The doctor said, "Well, you don't have cancer, "and closed the book. I said to her, I know that, but was cancer found? She opened the book again, looked, and looked said no, but you did have cancer. With a big smile on my face, I said, "I know God healed me." I was very happy, but I heard God telling me something else, and the healing wasn't all. I came outside from the hospital and told my husband, who was waiting outside. I felt like God was saying this is not the end of the miracle. I called my pastor and told him we were coming to see him and first lady. We had something to tell them. Remember, no one knew. We got there and related the testimony to them. I told them I felt like that's not the end of the testimony, but I didn't say what God had said. My husband turned and said God might give me back a new womb, we all laughed, and that was that.

There was a conference in Maryland two weeks later with Apostle Johnson Sulemon, who had prophesied about my healing. He also located me and called me by my name 3 years before and told me exactly why I was there, and true to what he said, God came through. I went there to testify, but to my surprise, the first session in the morning, he called out there was a woman there who they just removed her womb. God said He is replacing it with a new one. Let me tell you something! I was stunned. Yes, I was, but remember, God had told me so. I didn't go there expecting to hear that, but it confirmed what God said. I don't know who needs to hear this, but God is still doing creative miracles today. This is not for me, I believe, but for everyone reading this book, I am almost 60 years old. I don't need a womb at this stage of my life. I am done with childbearing; I already have 5 children and 10 grandchildren. God wants his children and people, in general, to know he is still in the miracle business. I know there is a great God who heals, and this is my message. Like Pastor Jerry Eze would say, "What God cannot do does not exist." I am a strong believer in that. God didn't have to do anything for me to believe I know who he is, and I know how great he is, but for Him to do this miracle for me, it's a privilege. I am honored that God chose me to have mercy and to showcase His healing and I'm ready to tell the world.

14

WORSHIP YOUR WAY TO HEALING

JEHOVAH QANNA – Do not worship any other god, for the Lord whose name is Jealous, is a jealous God.

In our Christian walk we are to be very careful not to be carried away with God's grace and mercy but forget that God is a jealous God. God will not come second to none, nor be anybody back up plan. We need to recognize that it doesn't have to be an object in a corner and someone kneeling there worshipping. It can be a small thing we are being more attentive to and spending more time with.

God will not share His glory with no one not ever.

If you know God and not only His works, it would be impossible to worship another or some mere image. God works how He pleases. If you don't know him, you can easily get impatient. The children of Israel when Moses took a long time to get back to them, they made an idol of gold to worship. How can you turn so quick to evil when you know and proven God? We were made to worship, if you're not worshipping God, you will worship something else. You may not be knowingly worshipping whatever it is but you are.

God main reason for creating this world is that His creation would worship Him. Worship rightfully belongs to God; He is not asking for something that does not belong to Him. Isaiah 42:8 [ESV] says I am the Lord; that is my name; My glory I give to no other, nor My praise to carved idols. Exodus 23:25 says Worship the Lord your God, and his blessing will be on your food and water. I will take away sickness from among you.

Check your life make certain there isn't anything God is trying to divert you from. Maybe where you are heading is not God intent for your life and He needs you to make an about turn. We see everything as the devil fighting us, but it can be God fighting to preserve his glory. God will remove anything that threatens to take His place and position in your life.

Study the life of King David, he was a worshipper, the way he worshipped God that God called him a man after His heart. How about that, who wouldn't want to be called a man or woman after God's heart? In most of the psalms of King David you can hear it being sang in today's worship. David just knew how to touch God's heart with adoration. He would tell God how wonderful He is. He told Him how beautiful the trees are, sky, mountains, hills and everything in between. David worshipped God as though he met Him face to face, the way he worshipped God, the extent of his love is felt in the Psalms.

God loves when we worship Him. If you are not worshipping God, you are worshipping something else. If you are not a believer and not a worshipper, you are in grave trouble. I can't stress how important it is for us to worship God. When we worship, we are instructed to worship God in spirit and in truth. God loves pure worship; it is easy when you know your God and when you look around to see you are still standing. How many people you know didn't make it? God has been good to you, don't mind the circumstances, worship Him for who He is. Look around and see there is something to worship God for.

Look at the sky, first worship Him because you can see, many have eyes but can't see. I remember driving on the new jersey turnpike every Friday, the sun bright, the sky beautifully blue and white, just perfect and I would think how awesome a creator my God is. I am writing this, and my eyes are welling up with tears. When I beheld the beauty of the scenery before me, it took me into worship for the next three sometimes four hours while driving. How great and creative is this God I thought? oh such an artist, see His handy works. For me worship comes easy, I love to worship this God that I serve. There are numerous people in this world, but he chooses me to worship Him. Why would I not? Can I find a bigger God somewhere? That has never crossed my mind, not to even think or look... This God that I serve is all I ever need, there is none other Hallelujah. No one can fully comprehend the majestic beauty of God's creation. He is too much.

15

MAINTAIN YOUR JOY

James 1: 2 admonish us to count it all joy when ye fall into divers' temptations; knowing this, that the trying of your faith worketh patience. I can say it was easy to maintain my joy, but the truth be told it wasn't. I have since come to realize that joy doesn't come from what's going on around me. Joy comes from deep within, it is given to us, it's a part of the kingdom of God. It is our duty to let it nourish us, we can suppress it, when we take on the negativities happening around us.

Let us be careful not to focus on sickness, bills or whatever present trouble we have. The bible says if we get into trouble, God delivers us from them all. Romans 12:12 says Be joyful in hope, patient in affliction, faithful in prayer. When there's an understanding of the hope we have, we are not just anybody we have hope in the healer, deliver, provider, what's your case again? He is the answer for that too.

The scripture says a cheerful heart is good medicine, but a crushed spirit dries up the bones. Proverbs 17:22. The heart is to be always guarded for out of it flows the issues of life. God gives us the answer here. Joy is good medicine, stay joyful even if its hard your body will absorb the joy and distribute healing to very part of your body. The joy of the Lord is our strength, the joy in you strengthens your body. Don't faint when there is adversary if you do then check your faith.

If you don't have joy you are defeated, maintain your joy. Delight yourself in the Lord and God will give you the desires of your heart. If your desire is to be healed, then you will be. You can receive so much if you learn to stay joyful. Where the presence of the Lord is, there is joy, there is peace for you to rest in the holy Ghost.

Look into the eyes of the spirit, see your healing or rather see you already healed. Never allow yourself to be downcast. You can be downcast if you are going according to feelings. God calls us to manifest His glory. Express your joy, joyfully, let it be contagious. Never let the devil rejoice over you. You have a weapon for every arrow, use it. God made us for His own pleasure, so He is not happy to see us unhappy. He loves cheerful children and loves to see us laugh, He himself laughs. God has a great sense of humor. I never go my Father in fear, I practice telling Him everything. I don't have a formal way to speak to my father, I talk to him anytime, anyplace, in my car, on my bed, it doesn't matter He is my Father, He loves me.

Reconnected with your joy, throw off the weight that easily beset you. Evoke the joy of the Lord, let the joy bubble in you. Rejoice because you have the greatest physician, and he is your Father. Encourage the presence of your Father when you are welcoming Him. I would not want to enter a home if the person that opens the door is not welcoming. Change your attitude, your mindset, become fierce, speak the word, encourage yourself. Finally count your blessings, name them one by one and it will surprise you what the Lord has done. If you had ten thousand tongues, it still wouldn't be enough to tell Him how great He is.

16

SOW SEEDS IT WILL GROW

Partner with an alter that is works for you. That alter must have evidence of the tangible working power of God. It should be a house of God where miraculous miracles are demonstrated. If you sow seed where there is no growth, no evidence of God's power, then expect the same. Sow seeds on fertile soil, let it grow and flourish. Make your seed noticeable to your God. Give until your giving beg you to stop.

Be a Barnabas in a ministry that has God's approval. Connect yourself be serious about funding the kingdom of God. Bless the Lord with your substance, He is not unrighteous to forget. If you have little then sow little, if you have much then sow much. Be actively involved with anything to do with building God's Kingdom. There was a good man name Joseph who was given the name Barnabas which means the encourager. He was a great help to the apostles.

Luke8:1-3 tells how women follow Jesus as he went throughout the country, visiting cities and villages to announce the wonderful news. The women that followed Jesus supported Him in ministry from their own personal finances also traveled with him.

How can you be about God's business and not receive His benefit? Seeds don't have to be money. It can be your time, giving to orphans, the homeless, the elderly that needs help. Take your mind off you, help others, maybe that's all it takes to get your answer.

17

MY MISSION

I am determined never to let this testimony go cold. If you can hear it and I'm in contact, you will hear it. I am not ashamed of my GOD, MY DELIVERER, my friend, my everything. I promised God I would testify and tell everyone I am in contact with. Don't get me wrong, God did a lot for me and still is doing a lot for me, but this is a testimony that can help so many people. All you hear lately is a whole lot of people dying of cancer. Cancer got a name that is bigger than itself, the thought of it makes people shiver, but I'm a living testimony that it is not a match to God, no match and God loves you enough to heal you. It is just the manifestation in your body. The Bible says ye were healed. To that patient, on the cross is where your healing took place, speak it, declare it is done. Many are the afflictions of the righteous, but God delivers us from them all. I learned you have to be patient and that you cannot rush God. People say God is always on time. I say God himself is time, and things get done on his time. We have to come into his time and learn to wait in Praise. If we can get in our soul the word, then we will be able to conquer anything, let what's in our soul match up with what our mouth speaks.

Let me encourage someone today. There is a God. There is a God who loves you and is waiting to have a conversation with you. He is better than any friend, any job, whatever is dear to you. God is too faithful to fail you. He wants to make you a wonder. He is a friend worth having. To someone reading this book today who already accepted Jesus and you are believing God for healing or something else. Just know you are already a winner; you are victorious on the winning side. His promises are yes and amen. He cannot be corrected because He is not man. He does not make mistakes. Don't let fear cause you an early death. Encourage yourself in the Lord. Have confidence in Him. He has begun a good work in you and is able to finish it. Give him a chance. He loves you.

I have countless testimonies about how God delivered not only me but my family too. I just feel led to share this testimony of what God did for my mom years ago. My mom was scheduled for an eye operation. She had glaucoma, which was seriously damaging her eyesight. The night before the surgery, she said she felt like someone was scraping in her eyes, and it was so bad she couldn't sleep. She went early in the morning to the hospital, and as they were prepping her for the surgery, the doctor ordered another test before he operated. To the doctor's surprise, there was no need for surgery. My mother's eyes were completely healed. My mom started reading that day with no reading glasses until she died at 83 years old. My mom believed in God for everything. She was truly a believer and knew her God, for which I'm thankful.

Who needs a miracle today? Who needs a creative miracle? Jehovah can do that too. Is there anything too hard for Your God? Then try mine; he is asking you today, is there anything too hard for me? Behold, he is the God of all flesh. He is a God that you can stand on his word with all confidence of not being put ashamed. Trust and believe that. AMEN, AMEN, AMEN! IT IS SO! IT IS SO! Hallelujah!!!!

CONFESSION

I see my healing through the eyes of faith.

I know whose I am, and what body I carry.

The power of God dominates over all deceases, sickness and afflictions.

I am made from the very essence of God.

I am equal with divinity.

My health is aligned to the word of God.

My blood, every cell, tissue. Bone and vein, align right now with the word of God.

I decree that I rule and reign over every sickness and disease.

I am extraordinary, I refuse to accommodate any form of sickness and disease in my body.

I live, move and have my being in Him.

I walk in the true inheritance in Christ knowing my health is secure and guaranteed every day in Jesus' name.

Cancer cannot fine a home in my body.

Consuming fire burn every tumor, any strange bacteria or viruses trying to take up space in my body.

I put on incorruption, my body is immune to any form of cancer and infection in the mighty name of Jesus.

I say no to any negative report from doctors because they do not have a say in my life.

I have been empowered to live a new life in Christ.

I am seated in the heavenly place in Christ Jesus, where pain, illness, and mortality have no hold on me.

I enjoy abundant life that is granted to me in Jesus' name.

I have the DNA of Jesus Christ, and sickness is not found there.

God is my habitation; therefore, sickness cannot find me.

Because the blood of Jesus saturates my mind, body and spirit, there is no room for sickness and diseases.

I am redeemed from the power of the grave.

I speak today that the words I carry is power and life.

I declare I am preserved in health always.

HEALING CONFESSIONS

I reject ownership of any disease sicknesses and symptom that goes against Gods declaration of life health and prosperity for me.

I take my prosperity; devil you take your sickness and your disease in the mighty name of Jesus.

I am made entirely whole in my body, mind, and spirit because I serve a God of completion.

There is no lack in my being for I was formed in the image and likeness of God who is perfect. God word is our medicine.

I take held of the God Given life, I have received and choose to walk in health and wealth.

No one can take what God has given me, divine health is my birthright.

I decree and declare that I experience Heaven on earth in everything that concerns me, Heaven on earth in my health in the mighty name of Jesus.

I am born of Christ therefore supernatural health and strength are mine always.

I am like the palm trees in Lebanon.

LIFT YOUR EXPECTATIONS HIGH

Learn to meditate on the word. Spend time on the scripture, pray for the eyes of your understanding to enlightened Ephesians1:18

Expect to be protected by angels. Psalms 91:11

Expect to get out of that situation. Psalms48:2

Expect the doctor's report to change for the better. Isaiah 41:10

Expect to be healed when you pray in faith. James 5:15

Expect to see the end of the sickness and not the other way around. Matthew 11:28

Expect to hear the voice of God and you will hear Him. Psalms 91: 15

Expect to live and declare the works of the Lord. Psalms 91:16

Expect a miracle. Matthew 4:23-25

Psalms 23;6 says Surely goodness and mercy shall follow me all the days of my life. According to this scripture goodness and mercy not sickness and disease

shall follow you. Expect your outcome to be good and God mercy to prevail.

Psalms 23:3 Expect your soul to be restored.

ACKNOWLEDGMENTS

My heartfelt and profound gratitude goes to my Heavenly Father, who loves me so much and thought it best to perform this miracle for me. Not only that but as a bonus created a brand-new womb for me. I thank him for his grace and presence every time I write. I never thought about writing a book, but what do you know, God said it, I believed it, and that settled it. I actually can't believe it. Wow, it's done. To God alone be all the glory!

Like Paul said, I thank my God upon every remembrance of you, my husband, Keith. He has a spirit like Barnabas, the encourager. If I tell Keith I am going to the moon, he will believe I can do it. I am blessed and honored to have such a dedicated and such a loving husband who believes in me. Keith, I appreciate your support immensely. You are forever, my darling. I love you so much.

I thank my children and grandchildren, who believed in me and encouraged me along the way. I appreciate my siblings very much and the rest of my family. I say thank you for every word of encouragement. Love you all.

I appreciate my home church Brooklyn Miracle Temple, Pastor Jimmy Talton and First Lady Daisy Talton. Thank you for all the prayers and encouragement.

I couldn't do this without the help of my dearest sister in the Lord, Jennifer Francis. You were my coach, my editor, my encourager and really a destiny helper. I say a very big thank you. I love you, girl.

Thank you all very much. Love always.

www.ingramcontent.com/pod-product-compliance
Lightning Source LLC
LaVergne TN
LVHW010504160826
845677LV00012B/2655

* 9 7 9 8 9 8 8 3 1 8 1 0 1 *